Date:

Created especially for you

Date: _______________________________

Date:

Date: _______________________

Everyone needs
'A Little Black Book'.
A place to write 'secret
things' and to write 'stuff'
that you think about and
want to remember - and
not want to remember.
'A Little Black Book' is that
prized and treasured
notebook
that you keep close to your
heart.
The 'Little Black Book' that
takes you on journeys of
memories - and prepares
you for the next one.
Everything you need will be
in here.

Created especially for you.....

Date:

Date: ___________________________

Date:

Created especially for you

Date: _______________________

Created especially for you

Date: _______________________

Created especially for you

Date: _______________________________

Created especially for you

Date: _______________________

Created especially for you

Date: _______________________

Created especially for you

Date:

Date:

Date: _______________________

Date:

Created especially for you

Date:

Date:

Created especially for you

Date:

Created especially for you

Date: ____________________

Created especially for you

Date: _______________________

Date:

Date: ______________________

Created especially for you

Date: ___________________________

Created especially for you

Date:

Date:

Created especially for you

Date:

Date: _______________________

Created especially for you

Date:

Date:

Created especially for you

Date:

Date: _______________________

Date: ____________

Date:

Created especially for you

Date: _______________________________

Created especially for you

Date:

Date: ___________________________

Created especially for you

Date: ______________________________

Date: _______________

Date: _______________

Date:

Date:

Date:

Date:

Date: _______________________

Date: ____

Created especially for you

Date: _______________

Date: _______________

Date: ___________________________

Created especially for you

Date:

Date:

Date:

Date: _______________________

Date:

Date: ________________________

Date:

Date:

Date:

Date: _______________________________

Created especially for you

Date:

Date:

Date:

Created especially for you

Date: ____

Date:

Date:

Created especially for you

Date:

Date: _______________________

Created especially for you

Date:

Date:

Created especially for you

Date:

Date: ______________________

Created especially for you

Date:

Created especially for you

Date: ______________________

Created especially for you

Date:

Date: _______________________

Date:

Created especially for you

Date:

Created especially for you

Date:

Date: _______________________________

Created especially for you

Date:

Date:

Created especially for you

Date:

Date:

Date:

Date:

Created especially for you

Date: _______________

Date: ______________________________

Date: _______________

Date: _______________________________

Created especially for you

Date:

Date: _______________________

Created especially for you

Date:

Date: _______________________

Created especially for you

Date:

Date:

Date:

Date: ___________________________

Created especially for you

Date:

Date:

Date:

Date: _______________________________

Created especially for you

Date:

Created especially for you

Date:

Date:

Date:

Created especially for you

Date:

Date: ______________________

Created especially for you

Date:

Date: _______________________

Created especially for you

Date:

Date: ___________________________

Created especially for you

Date:

Date: _______________

Date:

Date: ____________________________

Date: ____________________________________

____

____

____

____

____

____

____

____

____

____

____

____

____

____

____

Created especially for you

Date:

Date:

Date: ______________________________

Created especially for you

Date:

Date:

Date: _______________

Date:

Date:

Date:

Date:

Date:

Date: _______________

Date:

Created especially for you

Date:

Date:

Date: _______________________________

Created especially for you

Date: _______________

Date:

Date:

Date: _______________________________

Created especially for you

Date:

Created especially for you

Date: _______________

Date:

Date:

Date: _______________

Created especially for you

Date:

Date:

Date: ________________________

Created especially for you

Date:

Date: _______________

Date:

Date: _______________________________

Created especially for you

Date:

Created especially for you

Date: ________________________________

Created especially for you

Date: ________________

Date: _______________________

Created especially for you

Date: _______________

Date: ___________________________

Created especially for you

Date:

Date:

Date:

Date: _______________

Date:

Date: ___________

Created especially for you

Date:

Created especially for you

Date:

Date:

Date: ______________________

Date:

Date: _______________________________

Date:

Created especially for you

Date: _______________________________

Created especially for you

Date:

Date: _______________

Date:

Date:

Date:

Created especially for you

Date:

Date:

Date: _______________________________

Created especially for you

Date:

Date:

Created especially for you

Date:

Created especially for you

Date: ____

Created especially for you

Date:

Date:

Created especially for you

Date:

Date:

Created especially for you

Date:

Created especially for you

Date:

Created especially for you

Date:

Date: _______________________

Date:

Date: _______________________________

Created especially for you

Date: _______________

Created especially for you

Date: ___________________________

Created especially for you

Date:

Date: ___________________________

Created especially for you